supermom

supermom

inspirational words on motherhood

edited by siân keogh

Dedicated to the memory of my Mother.

Published in the United States in 2007
by Tangent Publications
an imprint of
Axis Publishing Limited
8c Accommodation Road
London NW11 8ED
www.axispublishing.co.uk

Creative Director: Siân Keogh
Editorial Director: Anne Yelland
Designer: Simon de Lotz
Production Manager: Jo Ryan

© 2007 Axis Publishing Limited

ISBN 978-1-904707-48-6

9 8 7 6 5 4 3 2 1

Printed and bound in Thailand

about this book

She is the most important person in the world. No matter how old you grow, you never outgrow your need for your mother's love, help, and support. This collection of wise and witty phrases and sayings on the joys of motherhood is the ideal gift book for your mom. With amusing animal photographs to complement the inspirational words, the book will raise a smile, offer food for thought, and generally let your mom know how much you love her and value everything she has done—and continues to do—for you.

about the author

Siân Keogh has worked in publishing for several years, and worked on titles across a wide variety of subjects. From the many hundreds of contributions that were sent to her, including some from her own children, she has selected the ones that best sum up the joys of motherhood.

Mom is as kind and
gentle as warm rain.

You have a lifetime
to work, but your kids
are only young once.

Mom, you're a poem
I'll never be able to write.

Mom, you're
strange and crazy,
and I love you.

A new baby is like the beginning
of all things—wonder, hope,
a dream of possibilities.

My mom has put a sign in
my room saying
"Checkout time is 18 years."

Mom is the one we count on for the things that matter most of all. She is food and bed and an extra blanket when it's cold.

Mom laughs my laughter
and shares my tears.

My mom's guess is more accurate than my dad's certainty.

Mom, you're the most
beautiful person I ever saw.

Mom is the pivot on
which the family spins.

Mom, you're a star.

A baby is born with a need to be loved and never outgrows it.

Mom, you're the
truest friend I have.

My mother is a saint.

Your heart always understands
when I need a friend.

Life began with waking
up and seeing my
mom's face.

Mom, you are
my sunshine when
the sun doesn't
show up.

Your kids don't need
all you can afford
to give them.

My mother's love is peace.

My mother loves me and will love me for ever with an affection which no chance, no misery, no crime of mine can diminish.

Moms keep finger paintings, clay pots, painted Easter eggs, and report cards.

My mother's love is the almond blossom of my mind.

What the mother
sings to the cradle
goes all the way
down to the coffin.

Love begins and ends
with my mom.

Momma, your gentle
eyes become stern when
I need a lesson.

Mom, you're there when troubles thicken all around me.

Mom knows that the way to bring up children is to spend half as much money and twice as much time on them.

What feeling is so nice as
a child's hand in yours?

A mom's pleasure is
her kids' happiness.

It's not what you do for your kids that counts, it's what you teach them to do for themselves.

Moms make homes.

Children are the anchors
that hold a mother to life.

Only a mother knows
a mother's fondness.

Mom is my bridge,
holding steady for me.

I'll never forget the stories Mom told me.

Moms kiss tears dry.

Love begins and ends
with motherhood.

A sweet child is the sweetest thing in Nature.

Mom, every day I thank
God for blessing me with
a mother like you.

Home is where my mother is.

Mom would give me the whole world if she could gather it in her arms.

Anyone can be a mother,
but it takes someone
special to be a mom.

I never knew how much love my heart could hold until someone called me "mommy."

If everyone had a mom half as wonderful as my mom, they would be blessed.

Mom, you will be a part
of everything I do.

Moms carry the keys of our souls in their bosoms.

Only a mom as perfect as you,
could have a kid as perfect as me.

My mom's not human…

…she's an angel.

My hope and faith and pride
are all from you, Mom.

If I had a flower for
each time I think of you,
Mom, I could walk
in a garden forever.

A mother's love
endures through all.

Mom, to the world you are one person, but to me you are the world.

Mom, my roots are in your heart.

My mother's love is peace.

There's no rose as lovely
as my mother's smile.

Mom listens to all my problems, even if I don't always listen back.

Mom, you're my daycare, chauffeur, maid, cook, and gardener…

…and I love you.

Mom, you made me what I am…

…congratulations.

Mom, you're a superhero.